THE AWESOME BOOK OF

Heavenly Humor

BOB PHILLIPS

CARTOONS BY JONNY HAWKINS

HARVEST HOUSE™ PUBLISHERS

EUGENE, OREGON

Cover by Terry Dugan Design, Minneapolis, Minnesota

THE AWESOME BOOK OF HEAVENLY HUMOR
Copyright © 2003 by Bob Phillips & Jonny Hawkins
Published by Harvest House Publishers
Eugene, Oregon 97402

ISBN 0-7369-1091-3

Harvest House Publishers has made every effort to trace the ownership of all quotes. In the event of a question arising from the use of a quote, we regret any error made and will be pleased to make the necessary correction in future editions of this book.

Printed in the United States of America.

05 06 07 08 09 10 11 /BC-KB / 10 9 8 7

Moses beats around the burning bush.

©2000 Jonny Hawkins

A

Abel

Question: What caused Abel to feel neglected?

Answer: His parents were raising Cain.

Absalom

Question: What did David think of the behavior of his son Absalom?

Answer: He thought it was revolting.

Active

Visitor: Pastor, how many of your members are active?

Pastor: They all are! Some are active for the Lord, and some are active for the devil!

Adam and Eve

The only things Adam would recognize if he came back to earth would be the jokes.

ⓖ ⓖ ⓖ

What a good thing Adam had. When he said something new, nobody had said it before.

Adam's rib on the eve of Eve

©2001 Jonny Hawkins

Adam may have had his troubles, but at least he didn't have to listen to Eve talk about the man she could have married.

⊚ ⊚ ⊚

Eve: Adam, do you love me?

Adam: Who else?

⊚ ⊚ ⊚

Adam and Eve lived thousands of years B.C. (Before Clothing).

@ @ @

Adam and Eve in the Garden of Eden couldn't complain how much better things were in the good old days.

@ @ @

Even Adam and Eve had their problems. One day Adam got angry. "You've done it again, Eve," he said. "You put my shirt in the salad!"

@ @ @

Adam and Eve lived together in Paradise—not once did Eve ask Adam to take out the garbage.

@ @ @

Eve was the first woman who ever said, "I haven't got anything to wear," and meant it!

@ @ @

Weary salesclerk: "Did you ever wonder how many fig leaves Eve tried on before she said, 'I'll take this one'?"

"Actually, you don't know of any good bed and
breakfasts around here, do you?"

The day the Pilate light was out

©2002 Jonny Hawkins

Question: What was the telephone number in the Garden of Eden?

Answer: I think it was Adam—8-1-2.

Question: How were Adam and Eve prevented from gambling?

Answer: They had their Paradise taken away.

◎ ◎ ◎

Question: Who was the fastest runner in the world?

Answer: Adam—he was first in the human race.

◎ ◎ ◎

Question: What did Adam and Eve do when they were expelled from Eden?

Answer: They raised Cain.

◎ ◎ ◎

Question: What did Adam say to Eve during one of their arguments?

Answer: "Don't forget who wears the plants in this family!"

◎ ◎ ◎

Question: Who introduced the first walking stick?

Answer: Eve—when she presented a little Cain to Adam.

◎ ◎ ◎

Camel Lot in the Bible

©2001 Jonny Hawkins

The little rich girl came back from her first trip to Sunday school and told her mother, "Oh, Mummy! They read us the nicest story about a Mr. Adam and a Miss Eve and what a nice time they were having under an apple tree until a servant came along and disturbed them."

"I don't know about the land of milk and honey, but maybe we could go somewhere with coffee and donuts."

©2001 Jonny Hawkins

Sam: My daddy has Washington's sword and Lincoln's hat.

Bill: That's nothing. My father has an Adam's apple.

@ @ @

Question: What did Adam never have but still provide for his children?

Answer: Parents.

When fighting the Amalekites, Moses had confidence in his God, his men, and his deodorant.

©2001 Jonny Hawkins

A Sunday school teacher asked her class to draw a picture illustrating a Bible story. Little Johnny drew a picture of a big car. An old man was driving, his long whiskers flying in the breeze. A man and a woman were seated in the back of the car. Puzzled, the teacher asked Johnny to explain his drawing. "That's God. He's driving Adam and Eve out of the Garden of Eden."

ⓖ ⓖ ⓖ

Sunday school teacher: Can anyone tell me the story of Adam and Eve?

Little girl: First God created Adam. Then He looked at him and said, "I think I could do better if I tried again." So He created Eve.

ⓖ ⓖ ⓖ

Question: What is the first theatrical event in the Bible?

Answer: Eve's appearance for Adam's benefit.

ⓖ ⓖ ⓖ

Question: At what time of day was Adam born?

Answer: A little before Eve.

@ @ @

Question: Why did Eve have no fear of the measles?
Answer: Because she'd Adam.

**"Thanks for the name. The platypus, dung beetle,
and I have already begun group therapy."**

©2001 Jonny Hawkins

ⓖ ⓖ ⓖ

Question: Why was Adam's first day the longest?
Answer: Because it had no Eve.

ⓖ ⓖ ⓖ

A little girl reported at home what she had learned at Sunday school concerning the creation of Adam and Eve: "The teacher told us how God made the first man and the first woman. He made man first. But the man was very lonely with nobody to talk to him. So God put the man to sleep. And while the man was asleep, God took out his brains and made a woman out of them."

ⓖ ⓖ ⓖ

Question: Who was created first, Adam or Eve?
Answer: Eve. She was the first maid.

ⓖ ⓖ ⓖ

A Sunday school teacher asked little Willie who the first man in the Bible was.

"Hoss," said Willie.

"Wrong," said the teacher. "It was Adam."

"Ah, shucks!" Willie replied. "I knew it was one of those Cartwrights."

"Perhaps you would've stayed afloat if you
were a little boulder."

©2001 Jonny Hawkins

◎ ◎ ◎

Sunday school teacher: Class, what do you know about
Adam's wife, Eve?

Student: They named Christmas Eve after her.

"No, no no...the Bible doesn't say 'Put on the whole <u>armadillo</u> of God.'"

©2000 Jonny Hawkins

Surgeon: I think the medical profession is the first profession mentioned in the Bible. God made Eve by carving a rib out of Adam.

Engineer: No, engineering was first. Just think of the engineering job it was to create things out of chaos.

Politician: That's nothing . . . who do you think created chaos?

⊚ ⊚ ⊚

After hearing the story about how God took the rib out of Adam's side, a little boy who had been running and had gotten a side ache told his mother, "I think I'm going to have a wife."

Air-conditioned

"Our church should be air conditioned," snapped Mrs. Smith. "It is unhealthy for people to sleep in a stuffy room."

Agnostic

An agnostic is a learned man who doesn't pretend to know what ignorant men are sure of.

⊚ ⊚ ⊚

Agnostic: Christians should stop building such large and fancy buildings and give the money to the poor.

Christian: I've heard that remark before.

Agnostic: By whom, may I ask?

Christian: Judas Iscariot.

Amen

We've been letting our six-year-old go to sleep listening to the radio, and I'm beginning to wonder if it's a good idea. Last night he said his prayers and wound up with: "And God bless Mommy and Daddy and Sister. Amen—and FM!"

**The common adornment for biblical warriors:
camelflage.**

©2001 Jonny Hawkins

"Heavy Metal" in the Bible

©2001 Jonny Hawkins

🌀 🌀 🌀

The sermon went on and on and on, and the church got warmer and warmer. At last the minister paused and asked, "What more, my friends, can I say?"

In the back of the church a voice offered earnestly: "Amen!"

ⓢ ⓢ ⓢ

Mack: Why do you say "Amen" in a church instead of "Awomen"?

Jack: Because you sing hymns, not hers.

ⓢ ⓢ ⓢ

The new Army recruit was given guard duty at 2 A.M. He did his best for a while, but at about 4 A.M. he went to sleep. He awakened to find the officer of the day standing before him.

Remembering the heavy penalty for being asleep on guard duty, this smart young man kept his head bowed for another moment and looked upward and reverently said, "A-a-a-men!"

Amusement

Henry Ward Beecher asked Park Benjamin, the poet and humorist, why he never came to hear him preach. Benjamin replied, "Why, Beecher, the fact is I have conscientious scruples against going to places of amusement on Sunday."

Angels

God made man a little lower than the angels, and men have been getting a little lower ever since.

—Will Rogers

Moses is a basket case.

©2001 Jonny Hawkins

ⓖ ⓖ ⓖ

A woman who is always up in the air and harping on something is not necessarily an angel.

Apocryphal

Hippety-hop to the corner shop for apocryphal of candy.

"And today's forecast calls for showers of blessings
in the east, the risen Son all about, and many
in the heartland surrounded by so great
a cloud of witnesses..."

©2001 Jonny Hawkins

Appropriate

It was a formal banquet. The minister had just finished saying grace when a waiter spilled a bowl of steaming soup into his lap. The clergyman silently sizzled, then said in anguished tones, "Will some layman please make some appropriate remarks!"

Armageddon

As St. John said after his dream, "Armageddon out of here!"

ⓖ ⓖ ⓖ

Ad in newspaper:

Armageddon—The Earth's Last War—How and Where It Will Be Fought at the First Baptist Church.

Art

"It's no use. Art doesn't listen to me," said a little boy who was praying for a new bike.

"Art who?" asked the boy's mother.

"Art in heaven," came the reply.

Atheist

An atheist is one who hopes the Lord will do nothing to disturb his disbelief.

—Franklin P. Jones

Blind Bartimaeus Is Healed

©2001 Jonny Hawkins

An atheist is a man who has no invisible means of support.

Have you heard about the dial-a-prayer service for atheists? You call a number and nobody answers.

௫ ௫ ௫

CHERRY IN THE PITS

Non-fruits of the Spirit

©2000 Jonny Hawkins

To be an atheist requires an infinitely greater measure of faith than to receive all the great truths which atheism would deny.

—Joseph Addison

ⓖ ⓖ ⓖ

One of the quirks of owning a serpent/staff

©2001 Jonny Hawkins

No atheist can injure the Bible's influence so
thoroughly as can a Christian who disregards it in
his daily life.

⊚ ⊚ ⊚

When you serve an atheist a meal, ask him if he
believes there is a cook.

⊚ ⊚ ⊚

Did you hear about the son of atheists who asked his
parents, "Do you think that God knows we don't
believe in Him?"

⊚ ⊚ ⊚

Overheard: "I'm an atheist, thank God."

⊚ ⊚ ⊚

Atheists are sometimes really on the spot—they have
to sing "Hmmmmmmm bless America."

⊚ ⊚ ⊚

Sign on the tomb of an atheist:

Here lies an atheist. All dressed up and no place to
go.

⊚ ⊚ ⊚

The three great apostles of practical atheism that
    make converts without persecuting, and retain
    them with without preaching, are health, wealth,
    and power.

                                    —Charles Caleb Colton

                    ☺ ☺ ☺

Atheism is rather in the life than in the heart of a man.
                                    —Frances Bacon

                    ☺ ☺ ☺

Atheism is the death of hope, the suicide of the soul.

                    ☺ ☺ ☺

Some of the people who constantly talk the most about
    God are those who insist that He doesn't exist.

                    ☺ ☺ ☺

 Some are atheists only in fair weather.

                    ☺ ☺ ☺

I feel sorry for an atheist who needs help. Do they
    pray to Darwin?

A team of oral surgeons labored intensely for hours in one final effort to tame Kordell's tongue.

©2001 Jonny Hawkins

Attitude

Question: What kind of attitudes did Jesus appreciate in His disciples?

Answer: Beatitudes.

Awake

Many churches are now serving coffee after the sermon. Presumably this is to get the people thoroughly awake before they drive home.

Romans roadkill

©2001 Jonny Hawkins

B
~~~

Babel

Around the Tower of Babel was a din of iniquity.

Bad Day

You know it's going to be a bad day and you need to pray when:

You call Suicide Prevention and they put you on hold.

You turn on the news and they're showing emergency routes out of the city.

Your twin sister forgets your birthday.

You see a *60 Minutes* news team waiting in your office.

Your birthday cake collapses from the weight of the candles.

While following a group of Hell's Angels, you tap your horn accidentally and it sticks.

Belief

A preacher once asked an actor why the actor had such large audiences and the preacher had only a small congregation.

"I act as if I believe what I say," said the actor. "You preach as if you don't believe what you proclaim."

©2001 Jonny Hawkins

🌀 🌀 🌀

Agnostic philosopher Bertrand Russell was asked if he was willing to die for his beliefs. He replied, "Of course not. After all, I may be wrong."

🌀 🌀 🌀

Belly Button

Bill: How do babies get their belly buttons?

Susie: Well, when God finishes making little babies, He lines them all up in a row. Then he walks along in front of them. He pokes each one in the tummy with His finger and says, "You're done...you're done...you're done..."

Better Work

"Daddy, did God make you?"

"Yes."

"Did He make me?"

"Yes."

"I guess He's doing better work now."

Bible

Some family Bibles are passed down from generation to generation because they get so little wear.

The Scriptures teach us the best way of living, the noblest way of suffering, and the most comfortable way of dying.

—John Flavel

Most people are bothered by those passages of Scripture they do not understand, but the passages that bother me are those I do understand.

—Mark Twain

@ @ @

The one who samples the Word of God occasionally never acquires much of a taste for it.

@ @ @

The Bible is a window in this prison world, through which we may look into eternity.

—Timothy Dwight

@ @ @

Nobody ever outgrows Scripture; the book widens and deepens with our years.

—Charles Spurgeon

@ @ @

It is an awful responsibility to own a Bible.

@ @ @

©2000 Jonny Hawkins

Be careful how you live; you may be the only Bible
some person ever reads.

⑤ ⑤ ⑤

People do not usually reject the Bible because it contradicts itself but because it contradicts them.

⑤ ⑤ ⑤

"Jesus said if any body part offends, get rid of it.
Be honest, do my feet offend you?"

©2001 Jonny Hawkins

Sin will keep you from this Book. This Book will keep
you from sin.

—Dwight L. Moody

☺ ☺ ☺

Johnny: Mother's Bible must be more interesting than
yours.

Father: Why do you say that?

Johnny: She reads hers more than you read yours.

ⓖ ⓖ ⓖ

"Why do you keep reading your Bible all day long?" a
　youngster asked his grandfather.

"Well," he explained, "you might say I am cramming for
　my final examinations."

Bingo

I've always been fascinated by churches that run bingo
　games. They ought to have a sign that says Come
　Let Us Prey.

Blindness

During church services an attractive young widow
　leaned too far over the balcony and fell, but her
　dress caught on a chandelier and held her
　suspended in midair. The minister, of course,
　immediately noticed the woman's predicament and
　called out to his congregation, "The first person
　who looks up is in danger of being punished with
　blindness."

One old fellow in the congregation whispered to the
　man next to him, "I think I'll risk one eye."

Boaz

Question: Why did those who worked for Boaz think
　he was a mean boss?

Answer: He became Ruthless when his wife went on
　vacation.

©2002 Jonny Hawkins

Bookie

Pastor: How do you like your job as church librarian?

Librarian: It's all right as long as people call me a librarian and not a bookie.

Bored

After a long, dry sermon, the minister announced that he wished to meet with the church board after the service. The first man to arrive was a stranger.

"You misunderstood my announcement. This is a meeting of the board," said the minister.

"I know," said the man. "If there is anyone here more bored than I am, I'd like to meet him."

Bridegroom

The bridegroom, who was in a horribly nervous condition, appealed to the clergyman in a loud whisper at the close of the ceremony:

"Is it kisstomary to cuss the bride?"

The clergyman replied:

"Not yet, it's a little too soon."

Buddhist

A Buddhist nudist is one who practices yoga bare.

Building Fund

I'm always suspicious of any church that tells you the end is near—and then asks you to sign a three-year building fund pledge.

"You can always tell when a Pharisee swallows a camel—by the hump in the throat."

©2001 Jonny Hawkins

C

~~~

Cain

Question: Why did Cain have a hard time making his parents happy?

Answer: He wasn't Abel.

Ⓖ Ⓖ Ⓖ

Question: What was the reason Cain didn't bring God the proper sacrifice?

Answer: He wasn't Abel.

Cannibals

A resourceful missionary fell into the hands of a band of cannibals. "I suppose you're going to eat me," said the missionary. "Actually, you wouldn't like me."

He took out his pocketknife, sliced a piece from the calf of his leg, and handed it to the chief. "Try it and see for yourself," he urged. The chief took one bite, grunted, and spat.

The missionary remained on the island 50 years. He had a wooden leg.

Christian

If a man cannot be a Christian in the place where he is, he cannot be a Christian anywhere.

—Henry Ward Beecher

Nobody can teach you how to be a Christian—you learn it on the job.

Methuselah, the early years

©2001 Jonny Hawkins

"I made it out of pray dough."

©2002 Jonny Hawkins

☺ ☺ ☺

A Christian is like ripening corn; the riper he grows the more lowly he bends his head.

☺ ☺ ☺

A Christian must carry something heavier on his shoulders than chips.

ⓢ ⓢ ⓢ

Christian: One who believes that the New Testament is a divinely inspired book admirably suited to the spiritual needs of his neighbors.

ⓢ ⓢ ⓢ

If Christians would really live according to the teachings of Christ, as found in the Bible, all of India would be Christian today.

—Mahatma Gandhi

ⓢ ⓢ ⓢ

Christian names are everywhere; Christian men are very rare.

Christianity

The trouble with some of us is that we have been inoculated with small doses of Christianity, which keep us from catching the real thing.

Christmas

Christmas began in the heart of God. It is complete only when it reaches the heart of man.

ⓢ ⓢ ⓢ

Christmas card from a mortgage lender:

Merry Christmas from our house to our house.

@ @ @

QUESTIONS TODAY'S KIDS WOULD ASK BIBLE CHARACTERS

"What was it like to live in Jesus' day... and why are you still in your bathrobe?"

©2001 Jonny Hawkins

I don't want to say that Christmas trees are expensive, but I bought one for 25 dollars. My wife is wearing it for a corsage.

❀ ❀ ❀

Some people call running a marathon good exercise. Others call it Christmas shopping.

❀ ❀ ❀

Jingle bells
Spending swells
Charge cards all the way.
Oh, what fun it is to shop,
Until you have to pay.

❀ ❀ ❀

"For Christmas," a woman remarked to her friend, "I was visited by a jolly, bearded fellow with a big bag over his shoulder. It was my son coming home from college with his laundry."

❀ ❀ ❀

There's nothing like the Christmas season to put a little bounce in your checkbook.

❀ ❀ ❀

John votes himself off the island of Patmos.

During a Christmas play: "Not a preacher was stirring, not even a mouse."

ⓖ ⓖ ⓖ

First it's December with Ho! Ho! Ho!
Then it's January with Owe! Owe! Owe!

ⓖ ⓖ ⓖ

Did you hear about the department store that had two Santas? One was an express line for kids who asked for nine toys or less.

ⓖ ⓖ ⓖ

A man goes through four stages:
    First, he believes in Santa.
    Later, he doesn't believe in Santa.
    Then, he is Santa.
    Finally, he looks like Santa.

Church

"Why don't you come to my church this next Sunday?"
"Because I belong to another abomination."

ⓖ ⓖ ⓖ

Church: A place where you encounter nodding acquaintances.

GRADES OF WRATH

Non-fruits of the Spirit

©2000 Jonny Hawkins

An usher went up to a man with his hat on in an old-fashioned church and asked him to remove it. "Thank goodness," said the man. "I thought that would do it. I've attended this church for months, and you are the first person who has spoken to me."

◎　◎　◎

"If absence makes the heart grow fonder," said a minister, "a lot of folks must really love our church."

◎　◎　◎

I don't want to say it was a cold church, but the ushers were using ice skates.

◎　◎　◎

I spoke in one church that was so small that when I took a bow, I hit my head on the back pew.

◎　◎　◎

The chief trouble with the church is that you and I are in it.

◎　◎　◎

Wife: Did you see that hat Mrs. Jones wore to church?

Husband: No!

Wife: Did you see the new dress Mrs. Smith had on?

Husband: No!

Wife: A lot of good it does you to go to church!

⊚ ⊚ ⊚

You can always tell a church that isn't doing well. The Cadillac they raffle off is a used one.

⊚ ⊚ ⊚

"The Bible says if I ask for an egg you won't give me a scorpion. So, if I ask for a nest egg you won't give me junk bonds?"

©2001 Jonny Hawkins

Churchgoer

Question: What do you call a non-churchgoer?

Answer: A Seventh-Day Absentist.

＠ ＠ ＠

"So if I understand it correctly, all the people in
the Bible dressed in flannelgraphs."

©2002 Jonny Hawkins

Church Members

Some church members who say "Our Father" on Sunday go around the rest of the week acting like orphans.

ⓢ ⓢ ⓢ

Every church has a brakeman, construction workers, and a wrecking crew. Which are you?

ⓢ ⓢ ⓢ

Every church has three classes of members: the workers, the jerkers, and the shirkers.

ⓢ ⓢ ⓢ

There are four classes of church members: the tired, the retired, the tiresome, and the tireless.

Church Signs

Come In and Let Us Prepare You for Your Finals

ⓢ ⓢ ⓢ

Let Us Take You to Our Leader

ⓢ ⓢ ⓢ

No Matter How Much You Nurse a Grudge It Won't
   Get Better

ⓖ   ⓖ   ⓖ

Pray Up in Advance

ⓖ   ⓖ   ⓖ

We Specialize in Faith Lifts

ⓖ   ⓖ   ⓖ

Ask About Our Pray-As-You-Go Plan

ⓖ   ⓖ   ⓖ

Merry Christmas to Our Christian Friends
Happy Hanukkah to Our Jewish Friends
To Our Atheist Friends...Good Luck!

ⓖ   ⓖ   ⓖ

Come Early If You Want a Back Seat

ⓖ   ⓖ   ⓖ

David and Bathsheba
> You've Seen the Movie
> Now Read the Book

◎ ◎ ◎

This Church Is Prayer Conditioned

◎ ◎ ◎

TO WHICH OF THESE DOES THE BIBLE REFER IN MARK 12?

1) DUST MITE

2) MIGHTY MITE

3) WIDOW'S MITE

©2000 Jonny Hawkins

An early member of the underground church

©2001 Jonny Hawkins

Cleanliness

Cleanliness is next to godliness, but in childhood it's next to impossible.

Cleopatra

Cleopatra was the queen of denial.

Clothes

Some clergymen preach against modern dress even though there's not enough left to talk about.

Coffee

Question: What is the clue that God may be a coffee drinker?

Answer: He brews.

Collection

A young clergyman, fresh out of seminary, thought it would help him in his career if he first took a job as a policeman for several months. He passed the physical examination and then took the oral examination to ascertain his alertness of mind and his ability to act quickly and wisely in an emergency. Among other questions he was asked, "What would you do to disperse a frenzied crowd?"

He thought for a moment and then said, "I would take up a collection."

Committees

If you want to kill any idea in the world today, get a committee working on it.

@ @ @

Never fear that machines may get too powerful. When they do, we can organize them into committees.

Rahab serves the spies a threadbare meal—soup on a rope.

©2001 Jonny Hawkins

ⓖ ⓖ ⓖ

A committee is a group that keeps minutes but loses hours.

Confession

Confess your sins to the Lord, and you will be forgiven; confess them to men, and you will be laughed at.

—Josh Billings

Confessional

Have you heard of the new drive-in confessional? It's called "Toot and Tell."

Consent

If thou wouldst conquer thy weakness, thou must never gratify it. No man is compelled to evil: his consent only makes it his. It is no sin to be tempted, but to be overcome.

—William Penn

Conscience

A good conscience is a continual Christmas.

—Benjamin Franklin

A guilty conscience is the mother of invention.

—Carolyn Wells

"I'm going to give you a prayscription. I want you to double your meditation and call on the Great Physician every morning."

©2001 Jonny Hawkins

Convention

The road to hell is paved with good conventions.

Cooks

Heaven sends us good meat but the devil sends us cooks.

—David Garrick

Country Parson

How to tell if you're a country parson: Do any of the items below apply to the members of your church?

If a member's front porch collapsed, would it kill more than six dogs?

Do your members think Spam on saltines is an hors d'oeuvre?

Do less than half of your members' cars run?

Have your members ever barbecued Spam on a grill?

Is the primary color of your members' cars "Bondo"?

Do your members have stuffed opossums somewhere in their houses?

Are the rear tires on your members' cars twice as wide as the front ones?

Do the diplomas of some of your members contain the words "Trucking Institute"?

Have the women in your church ever been involved in a fist fight at a high school sports event?

Do your members use rags for gas caps?

Do your members ever use a Weedeater indoors?

Do you have more than two members named Bubba or Junior?

Did any of your members quit high school because there was an opening on the lube rack?

Do your members prominently display souvenirs from Graceland?

Do your members think beef jerky and MoonPies are two of the major food groups?

Do the women in your church keep a spit cup on the ironing board?

The Prodigal Son wallows in his poverty by nearly making a pig of himself.

©2001 Jonny Hawkins

Jacob wrestles his conscience.

©2001 Jonny Hawkins

Do your members have toothpicks in their mouths in their wedding pictures?

Is the lifetime ambition of your members to own a fireworks stand?

If your richest member bought a new house, would you have to help take the wheels off?

When your members are asked to show their ID, do they show their belt buckles?

Do your members know exactly how many bales of hay
   their cars will hold?

Do your members have pink plastic flamingos in their
   yard not placed there as a joke?

Have any of your members ever broken a tooth
   opening a bottle of pop?

Do your members dress up to go to K-Mart or Wal-
   Mart?

Do your members include duct tape among the world's
   greatest inventions?

Do chewing tobacco companies ever send your
   members Christmas cards?

Criticize

When the family returned from Sunday morning
   service, father criticized the sermon, daughter
   thought the choir's singing was off-key, and
   mother found fault with the organist's playing.
   The subject had to be dropped when the small boy
   of the family said, "But it was a good show for a
   nickel, don't you think, Dad?"

"I gave my life to God while listening to you on the radio in my '67 Mustang...talk about a convertible!"

©2001 Jonny Hawkins

"Doc, if the operation isn't successful, I'll just get a first-hand second opinion from the Great Physician."

©2002 Jonny Hawkins

D

David

Question: How can you tell that David was older than Goliath?

Answer: David rocked Goliath to sleep.

Dead in Christ

One pastor said that his church people would be the first to go up in the Rapture. He gave his reason: "The Bible says, 'The dead in Christ shall rise first.'"

Defects

The defects of a preacher are soon spied.

—Martin Luther

Delilah

Question: What was the secret of Delilah getting into Samson's house?

Answer: She picked his locks.

ⓖ ⓖ ⓖ

Question: Why did Samson try to avoid arguing with Delilah?

Answer: He didn't want to split hairs.

Denominations

Question: When you have fifty people all of different opinions, what do you have?

Answer: A Methodist church.

 ⑥ ⑥ ⑥

"Some people say the Baptist denomination started with John the Baptist, but it was much earlier than that," said a great Baptist leader as he spoke to a large gathering of Baptist ministers. "In fact, it started way over in the Old Testament, in Genesis 13. Lot said to Abraham, 'You go your way and I'll go mine.' That's when the Baptists began."

⑥ ⑥ ⑥

A Baptist deacon had advertised a cow for sale.

"How much are you asking for it?" inquired a prospective purchaser.

"One hundred fifty dollars," said the advertiser.

"And how much milk does she give?"

"Four gallons a day," he replied.

"But how do I know that she will actually give that amount?" asked the purchaser.

"Oh, you can trust me," reassured the advertiser. "I'm a Baptist deacon."

"I'll buy it," replied the other. "I'll take the cow home and bring you back the money later. You can trust me, I'm a Presbyterian elder."

When the deacon arrived home he asked his wife, "What is a Presbyterian elder?"

"Oh," she explained, "a Presbyterian elder is about the same as a Baptist deacon."

"Oh, dear," groaned the deacon, "I just lost my cow!"

⑥ ⑥ ⑥

"Nazarene fellowship is heavenly."

"Yeah, heaven is the only place it will work."

"I'd love to enter the land flowing with milk and honey,
but I'm lactose intolerant."

©2001 Jonny Hawkins

"A dozen sinners following Jesus? Sounds like the original twelve-step group."

©2001 Jonny Hawkins

Depravity

Arriving home for the holidays from reform school, a teenage delinquent called out, "Look, Mom, no depravities!"

Devil

Where God builds a church, the devil builds a chapel next door.

—Martin Luther

An old Puritan said, "If you are a child of God and you marry a child of the devil, you will be sure to have trouble with your father-in-law."

The devil is never too busy to rock the cradle of a sleeping saint.

The devil's traps are never set in the middle of God's road.

Johnny: There's really no devil.

Billy: I know what you mean. Just like Santa Claus—it's really your father.

Talk of the devil, and his horns appear.

—Samuel Taylor Coleridge

Eve passes the fruit. God passes the judgment.
Adam passes the buck.

©2001 Jonny Hawkins

ⓖ ⓖ ⓖ

The devil is an artist. He paints sin in very attractive
  colors.

Devotions

Wife: Shall I wake you up when you finish your
  devotions, dear?

Died

Pastor: Isn't this a beautiful church? Here is a plaque for the men who died in the service.

Visitor: Which one? Morning or evening?

Discipline

A young businessman returned home after a tough day at the office and found his two daughters, both about kindergarten age, acting up pretty boisterously. He gave them a moderately severe scolding and sent them off to bed. The next morning he found a note stuck on his bedroom door:

"Be good to your children and they will be good to you. God."

Doctrine

Any doctrine that will not bear investigation is not a fit tenant for the mind of an honest man.

—Robert G. Ingersoll

Donkey

An evangelist was speaking in a meeting when a heckler shouted, "Listen to him! And his father used to drive a wagon led by a donkey."

"That's right," said the evangelist, "and today my father and the wagon are gone. But I see we still have the donkey with us."

Drowning

A prominent preacher was approached after Sunday morning services by an elderly lady who said in a tone of appreciation, "Bishop, you'll never know what your service meant to me. It was just like water to a drowning man!"

Drought

A visitor to a drought-stricken area was engaged in conversation at the local store about the no-rain situation.

"You think the drought is bad here," the merchant observed, "but down south of here a ways, they haven't had any rain for so long that the Baptists are sprinkling, the Methodists are using a damp cloth, and the Presbyterians are issuing rain checks!"

Dust

On the way home from church a little boy asked his mother, "Is it true, Mommy, that we are made of dust?"

"Yes, darling."

"And do we go back to dust again when we die?"

"Yes, dear. Why do you ask?"

"Well, Mommy, when I said my prayers last night and looked under the bed, I found someone who is either coming or going."

"I'm laying up treasures in heaven, and I'm starting by depositing this money into that cloud bank."

©2001 Jonny Hawkins

E

Elisha

A minister was talking to a Sunday school class about the familiar story of the children who mocked Elisha on his journey to Bethel. He shared how the youngsters taunted the poor old prophet and how they were punished. Two she-bears came out of the wild and ate 42 of them.

"And now, children," said the pastor, wondering whether he had gotten his point across, "what does this story show?"

A little girl in the front said, "It shows how many children two she-bears can hold."

Eloquence

God gave eloquence to some, brains to others.

Eutychus

Pastor: What do we learn from the story of Eutychus? Remember, he was the young man who, listening to the preaching of the apostle Paul, fell asleep. As a result, he fell out of a window and was taken up dead.

Member: Ministers shouldn't preach long sermons.

Evil

The greatest penalty of evildoing is to grow into the likeness of bad men, and growing like them, to fly from the conversation of the good, and be cut off from them, and cleave to and follow after the company of the bad.

—Plato

SHADRACH ON THE PSYCH'S COUCH

©2000 Jonny Hawkins

Faith

Minister: When in doubt, faith it.

False Teeth

At a Sunday school picnic the minister, while walking across a small footbridge, was seized with a fit of sneezing. His false teeth flew from his mouth and landed in the clear water in the middle of the stream. Much worried and embarrassed, the minister was preparing to remove his shoes and wade in after them.

A dear little gray-haired grandmother appeared on the scene, carrying a well-filled dinner basket. When she discovered the minister's plight, she reached into her basket. She removed a crisp, brown chicken leg, tied a string to it, and tossed it into the water near the dentures. Quickly the teeth clamped into the chicken leg and were hauled to safety.

Faults

Every person should have a special cemetery lot in which to bury the faults of friends and loved ones.

Fear

Fear is the tax that conscience pays to guilt.

And with one epic belch, Jonah becomes the original "dish to pass."

©2001 Jonny Hawkins

Fear the man who fears not God.

Fee

God cures, but the doctor takes the fee.

First Row

In a church where everybody sat toward the rear, a stranger walked in and took a front seat. After the service, the minister greeted the stranger and asked why he sat up front.

"I'm a bus driver," he replied, "and I came to learn how you succeed in getting people to move to the back."

—Josh Billings

Fishing

A village pastor, who had a weakness for trout, preached against fishing on Sunday. The next day one of his members presented him with a fine string of fish and said, hesitatingly, "I guess I ought to tell you, parson, that those trout were caught on Sunday."

The minister gazed appreciatively at the speckled trout, and said piously, "The fish aren't to blame for that."

Flirting

The minister arose to address his congregation. "There is a certain man among us today who is flirting with another man's wife. Unless he puts five dollars in the collection box, his name will be read from the pulpit."

When the collection plate came in, there were 19 five-dollar bills, and a two-dollar bill with this note attached: "Other three on payday."

Doubting Thomas' younger brother—Pouting Terrance

©2002 Jonny Hawkins

Flowers

Question: What do they do with the church flowers after Sunday services?

Answer: They take them to the people who are sick after the sermons.

Flying

Mother: You shouldn't be flying that model airplane in the backyard on Sunday.

Johnny: Oh, it's all right to fly this one. It isn't a pleasure plane. It's a missionary plane going to the jungle.

Fool

Reverend Henry Ward Beecher entered Plymouth Church one Sunday and found several letters awaiting him. He opened one and found it contained the single word, "Fool." Quietly and becoming serious, he announced to the congregation that fact in these words:

"I have known many an instance of a man writing a letter and forgetting to sign his name, but this is the only instance I have ever known of a man signing his name and forgetting to write the letter."

Foot in Mouth

A missionary was suddenly surrounded by hostile-looking tribesmen in a South American jungle. Noting their poised spears and poisoned arrows, he knew he had to think of something quickly. At that moment a plane flew overhead.

"See that bird up there?" said the missionary. "That's my friend. If you hurt me that bird will hurt you!"

The chief took one glance at the sky and then answered, "That's no bird. That's a Boeing 747!"

Forgiveness

It is easier for the generous to forgive than for the offender to ask for forgiveness.

ⓖ ⓖ ⓖ

Doing an injury puts you below your enemy, revenging one makes you but even with him, forgiving it sets you above him.

—Benjamin Franklin

ⓖ ⓖ ⓖ

"I can forgive, but I cannot forget," is only another way of saying, "I will not forgive."

Forgiveness ought to be like a cancelled note, torn in two and burned up so that it never can be shown against one.

—Henry Ward Beecher

ⓖ ⓖ ⓖ

"This couples' cruise was a great idea!"

©2000 Jonny Hawkins

It is easier to forgive an enemy than a friend.

ⓖ ⓖ ⓖ

There is no revenge so complete as forgiveness.

Freedom

Those who expect to reap the blessings of freedom
     must, like men, undergo the fatigues of supporting
     it.

—Thomas Payne

Funeral

A young minister, in the first days of his first parish,
     was obliged to call on the widow of an eccentric
     man who had just died. Standing before the open
     casket and consoling the widow, he said, "I know
     this must be a very hard blow, Mrs. Vernon. But we
     must remember, that what you see here is the
     husk only—the shell—the nut has gone to heaven."

G

~~~

Gas

Right in the middle of the service, and just before the sermon, a member of the congregation remembered she had forgotten to turn off the gas under the Sunday roast.

Hurriedly she scribbled a note and passed it to the usher to give to her husband, who was ushering in another part of the sanctuary. Unfortunately, the usher misunderstood her intention and took it to the pulpit.

Upon unfolding the note, the preacher read aloud, "Please go home and turn off the gas."

Gideon

Question: What did the men in Gideon's army think about their time of serving with him as a leader?

Answer: Torcher.

Gin

One priest to another, across the card table: "Forgive me, Father, for I have ginned."

Giving

A painter in California was asked to contribute to a drive being conducted by his church. "I'm broke," explained, "but I'll contribute a $500 picture."

When the drive was completed, the minister again contacted the painter explaining that the church was still $100 short of the goal. "OK," said the artist. "I'll increase the price of my picture to $600."

🌀 🌀 🌀

©2002 Jonny Hawkins

One reason we have so many pennies in the church collection plate is that we have no smaller coin.

◎ ◎ ◎

When it comes to giving, some people stop at nothing.

◎ ◎ ◎

Three men went to church, and when it came time to pass the plate, they discovered they had no money. Not wanting to be embarrassed, one fainted and the other two carried him out.

◎ ◎ ◎

The doctor sent a note to his minister: "Sorry I haven't tithed for three months. But you know, there's a lot of that going around."

◎ ◎ ◎

A minister habitually told his congregation to drop a note in the offering plate if they needed a pastoral visit. One evening after services he discovered a note that said: "I am one of your loneliest members and heaviest contributors. May I have a visit tomorrow evening?"

It was signed by his wife.

When Paul would get a letter back from the Ephesians

©2001 Jonny Hawkins

God has given us two hands—one to receive with and the other to give with. We are not cisterns made for hoarding; we are channels made for sharing.

—Billy Graham

God

Man: I'll give you a candy bar if you can tell me where God is.

Boy: I'll give you two candy bars if you can tell me where He isn't.

Golf

A distinguished clergyman and one of his parishioners were playing golf. It was a very close match, and at the last hole the clergyman teed up, addressed the ball, and swung his driver with great force. The ball, instead of sailing down the fairway, merely rolled off the tee and settled slowly some 12 feet away.

The clergyman frowned, glared, and bit his lip, but said nothing. His opponent regarded him for a moment, and then remarked:

"Reverend, that is the most profane silence I have ever witnessed."

Good

The man who says he is just as good as half the folk in the church seldom specifies which half.

Good for Nothing

Two boys were trying to outdo each other. The first said, "My uncle's a doctor. I can be sick for nothing!"

The second youngster shot back, "Big deal! My uncle is a preacher. I can be good for nothing!"

Good Medicine

Five-year-old Johnny was being urged by his mother to take some medicine.

"It's good for you, Johnny. And God wants you to take it."

"I don't think He does, Mommy. I'll ask Him." The youngster buried his head under the blankets on his bed, and soon a hoarse voice came. "No, definitely not!"

Goodness

No hell will frighten men away from sin, no dread of prospective misery; only goodness can cast hell out of any man and set up the kingdom of heaven within.

—Hugh R. Haweis

Good Samaritan

Sunday school teacher: In the story of the Good Samaritan, why did the Levite pass by on the other side?

Student: Because the poor man had already been robbed.

Gossip

"I think we need to change the morning hymn," said the minister to his song leader. "My topic this morning is gossip. I don't think 'I Love to Tell the Story' would be the best song."

"I'm all out of dough...do you take birthrights?"

Guard

It is too late to be on our guard when we are in the
    midst of evils.

—Seneca

@ @ @

SMART ALECKS AT THE RED SEA

©2000 Jonny Hawkins

H

Halo

St. Peter's greeting as you approach the gates: "Well, halo there."

Hay

One Sunday as a farmer was getting in his hay crop, his minister stopped by. The pastor asked the farmer if he had been to church. "To tell the truth, I would rather sit on the hay load and think about the church than sit in the church and think about hay."

Headache

Little Susie, a six-year-old, complained, "Mommy, I've got a stomachache."

"That's because your stomach is empty," her mother replied. "You'd feel better if you had something in it."

That afternoon the minister called, and in the conversation, he remarked he had been suffering all day with a severe headache.

Susie perked up. "That's because it's empty," she said "You'd feel better if you had something in it."

Heathen

After a special exhortation for support of foreign missions, the offering plate was passed. When it was presented to one man, he said to the usher, "I don't believe in missions."

"In that case," whispered the usher, "take something out—it's for the heathen."

Heaven

The distance from earth to heaven is not a matter of altitude but attitude.

◎ ◎ ◎

Almost everybody is in favor of going to heaven, but too many people are hoping they'll live long enough to see an easing of the entrance requirements.

◎ ◎ ◎

An exasperated mother, whose son was always getting into mischief, finally asked him, "How do you expect to get into heaven?"

The boy thought it over and said, "Well, I'll just run in and out and in and out and keep slamming the door until St. Peter says, 'For heaven's sake, Jimmy, come in or stay out.'"

Hell

Hell is full of good meanings and wishings.

—George Herbert

The man who tries to prove there is no hell generally
has a personal reason for doing so.

The feeding of the 5,000: the origin of Wonder Bread.

©2001 Jonny Hawkins

When a certain shameless fellow mockingly asked a pious old man what God had done before the creation of the world, the latter aptly countered that he had been building hell for the curious.

—John Calvin

◎ ◎ ◎

The trouble about dying and going below is, when you get mad at your friends, where do you tell them to go?

◎ ◎ ◎

A circuit rider, encountering many a meal that needed seasoning, carried with him a tiny bottle of Tabasco sauce. He would put it on the table before him at eating-houses.

A stranger, eyeing the bottle with curiosity, asked permission to try it. He put a liberal quantity on a piece of beef, and ate it. There was a pause.

The stranger (gulping down a glass of water) sputtered, "Say, parson, you preach hell, don't you?"

The circuit rider replied, "I feel it is my duty to remind the wicked that there is retribution beyond the grave."

The stranger replied, "Anyhow, you're the first preacher I've seen who carries samples!"

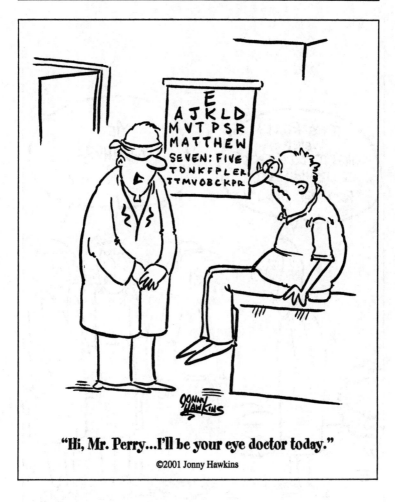

"Hi, Mr. Perry...I'll be your eye doctor today."

©2001 Jonny Hawkins

🌀 🌀 🌀

It doesn't matter what they preach,
Of high or low degree,
The old hell of the Bible
Is hell enough for me.

Shadrach, Meshach, and Abednego and aerobics

©2000 Jonny Hawkins

Hog Caller

A local pastor joined a community service club, and the members thought they would have some fun with him. Under his name on the badge they printed "Hog Caller" as his occupation.

Everyone made a big fanfare as the badge was presented. The pastor responded by saying, "I am usually called the 'Shepherd of the Sheep'...but you know your people better than I do."

Hymn

A distinguished theologian spoke to a Sunday school class for over two hours, and his remarks were too deep for the students to comprehend.

At the conclusion, the superintendent asked the class what hymn they would like to sing. Their unanimous choice: "Revive Us Again!"

◎ ◎ ◎

Three churches of different denominations were located on the same main intersection. One Sunday morning a passerby heard the first church singing, "Will There Be Any Stars in My Crown?"

The next church was singing, "No, Not One."

From the third church came, "Oh, That Will Be Glory for Me."

◎ ◎ ◎

What the world really needs is one more hymn: "I Did It Thy Way."

❂ ❂ ❂

Hypocrites

"I never go to church," boasted a wandering member. "Did you notice?"

"Yes, I noticed," said his pastor.

"Well, the reason I don't go is that there are so many hypocrites there."

"Oh, don't let that keep you away," replied the pastor, smiling blandly. "There is always room for one more, you know."

Hunting

A minister who paid more attention to hunting than to his sermons was taken to task by a parishioner.

"Pastor," said the parishioner, "I understand you're quite a hunter."

"One of the best," the minister replied complacently.

"If I were a deer," said the parishioner, "I would hide where you would never find me."

"Where would you hide?" asked the minister with a frown.

"In your study!"

"We heard there's an eternal wellspring around here somewhere. Know anything about it?"

©2001 Jonny Hawkins

Income Tax

Did you hear about the man from the IRS who phoned a certain Baptist minister to say, "We're checking the tax return of a member of your church. Mr. Smith lists a donation to your building fund of $5000. Is that correct?"

The minister answered without hesitation, "I haven't got my records available, but I'll promise you one thing: If he hasn't, he will!"

Isaiah

Question: Do you know what the name of Isaiah's horse was?

Answer: Is Me. Isaiah said, "Whoa, Is Me."

"If Moses never made it to the Promised Land, could he still join the Promise Keepers?"

©2001 Jonny Hawkins

J

Janitor

Pastor: How do you like your job?

Church janitor: It is a pushover. All I have to do is mind my keys and pews.

Jericho

Question: How did the people of Israel feel after walking around the walls of Jericho for seven days?

Answer: Week.

Jesus

Question: What kind of food did Jesus eat after fasting 40 days in the wilderness?

Answer: Fast food.

Job

"Did you know that Job spoke when he was a very small baby?"

"How do you know that?"

"The Bible says, 'Job cursed the day he was born.'"

Jonah

Question: How did the fish that swallowed Jonah obey the divine law?

Answer: Jonah was a stranger, and the fish took him in.

@ @ @

Question: Who was Jonah's tutor?

Answer: The fish that brought him up.

Joseph

Question: Who was the straightest man in the Bible?

Answer: Joseph. Pharaoh made a ruler out of him.

Joshua

Question: What man in the Bible had no parents?

Answer: Joshua, the son of Nun.

@ @ @

Question: What did the people of Israel think when Joshua told them the walls of Jericho would come tumbling down when they walked around them?

Answer: They thought he was Joshing.

Judas

Still as of old men by themselves are priced—
For thirty pieces Judas sold himself, not Christ.

—Hester M. Cholmondeley

Judgment

It is a sin to believe evil of another, but it is seldom a
  mistake.

—H.L. Mencken

"I'll have a whole lot of emptiness with a side of
nothing...and hold everything."

©2002 Jonny Hawkins

"Whatcha readin', Solomon?"

K
~~~

King Herod

A seminary class studied King Herod's dilemma when he offered up to half his kingdom to the daughter of Herodius.

"Now, what if you offered anything she wanted, and the girl came to you asking for the head of John the Baptist? If you didn't want to give it to her, what would you do?" asked the professor.

Soon a hand was raised. "I'd tell her," said one student, "that the head of John the Baptist was not in the half of the kingdom I was offering her."

©2002 Jonny Hawkins

"Now that all of us have trusted Christ,
this is our family tree."

©2001 Jonny Hawkins

L
~~~

Landlord

A big, burly man called at the pastor's home and asked to see the minister's wife—a woman well known for her charitable impulses.

"Madam," he said in a broken voice, "I wish to draw your attention to the terrible plight of a poor family in this district. The father is dead, the mother is too ill to work, and the nine children are starving. They will have to live on the streets unless someone pays their rent which amounts to $100."

"How terrible!" exclaimed the lady. "May I ask who you are?"

The sympathetic visitor applied his handkerchief to his eyes, "I'm the landlord," he said.

Last Words

The seven last words of the church: We never did it that way before.

Latin

Question: Name an outstanding feat of the Romans.

Answer: Speaking Latin.

©2000 Jonny Hawkins

Layman

A layman is someone who lays in bed Sunday morning instead of going to church.

LifeSaver

The sermons were always just 20 minutes in length. One day the preacher went an hour and 20 minutes. When asked why, he explained, "I always put a LifeSaver in my mouth and when it melts, I know the 20 minutes are up. But in my hurry, I put a button in my mouth by mistake!"

Lightbulb Changing

How many Southern Baptists does it take to change a lightbulb?

15,738,283, but they can't agree if it really needs to be changed.

How many campfire worship leaders does it take to change a lightbulb?

One, but soon all can warm up to its glowing.

How many Mennonites does it take to change a lightbulb?

Eventually about five, but they can get along fine without it.

How many televangelists does it take to change a lightbulb?

Only one, but for the light to continue burning, you need to send in your check today.

How many Mormon missionaries does it take to change a lightbulb?

Two. One to stand on the ladder while the other one rides his bike to the hardware store to get a bulb.

How many Episcopalians does it take to change a lightbulb?

Three. One to do it, one to bless the element, and one to pour the sherry.

How many Nazarenes does it take to change a lightbulb?

Eleven. One to change it and ten to organize the fellowship supper that follows.

How many Presbyterians does it take to change a lightbulb?

They're not sure, but there are several committees studying the issue.

How many members of the Church of Christ does it take to change a lightbulb?

Only one, but if anyone else tries to do it, the light won't come on.

How many Christian Scientists does it take to change a lightbulb?

Three. One to talk to the lightbulb and two to pray that the bulb will heal itself from within.

How many Methodists does it take to change a lightbulb?

Only one, but first they want to make sure no one will be offended by the change.

**At the Garden of Gethsemane, Jesus introduces
the first Miracle Ear.**

©2002 Jonny Hawkins

How many Catholics does it take to change a lightbulb?

> Nine. One to change it and eight to sell raffle tickets on the old bulb.

How many Charismatics does it take to change a lightbulb?

> Three. One to do it and two to bind the spirit of darkness.

How many Jehovah's Witnesses does it take to change a lightbulb?

> Two. One to change the lightbulb and one to hand you some literature to read first.

How many Amish does it take to change a lightbulb?

> What is a lightbulb?

Long-Winded

The new preacher at his first service had a pitcher of water and a glass on the pulpit. As he preached, he drank until the pitcher of water was completely gone.

After the service someone asked an old woman of the church, "How did you like the new pastor?"

"Fine," she said, "but he's the first windmill I ever saw that was run by water."

Lord's Prayer

A small boy, repeating the Lord's Prayer one evening, prayed:

"And forgive us our debts as we forgive those who are dead against us."

Loudspeaker

When dedicating the church's new public address
system, the pastor told the congregation that the
microphone and wiring had been paid for out of the
church funds. Then he added, "The loudspeaker
has been donated by a member of the congregation
in memory of his wife."

◎ ◎ ◎

"No, the <u>praying</u> mantis is down the lane a ways.
I'm the <u>meditating</u> mantis."

©2001 Jonny Hawkins

Lying

A minister wound up the services one morning by saying, "Next Sunday, I am going to preach on the subject of liars. As a preparation for my discourse, I would like you all to read Mark 17."

On the following Sunday, the preacher rose to begin, and said, "Now then, all of you who have read Mark 17 as I requested, please raise your hands."

Nearly every hand in the congregation went up. Then said the preacher, "You are the people I want to talk to. Mark has only 16 chapters."

"If I have the gift of celibacy, can I exchange it?"

©2001 Jonny Hawkins

M

~~~

Magi

Question: Where do the Magi go when they want to go on a vacation?

Answer: To the Magi Kingdom.

ⓖ ⓖ ⓖ

Question: How did one of the three wise men feel when his gift was rejected?

Answer: Incensed.

Mansions

The house of many mansions requires reservations in advance.

Martin Luther

A collector of rare books ran into an acquaintance of his who had just thrown away an old Bible that had been in his family for generations. He happened to mention that "Guten something" had printed it.

"Not Gutenberg?" gasped the book collector.

"Yes, that was the name."

"You idiot! You've thrown away one of the first books ever printed. A copy recently sold for $700,000 at an auction."

"Mine wouldn't have been worth a dime," replied the man. "Some clown by the name of Martin Luther had scribbled all over it."

Memory Verse

Sunday school teacher: Do you remember your memory verse?

Sunday school student: I sure do. I even remember the zip code—John 3:16.

Men's Fellowship

A letter to the men's fellowship read:

"All members are requested to bring their wives and one other covered dish to the annual banquet."

Minister

A minister was asked to inform a man with a heart condition that he had just inherited a million dollars. Everyone was afraid the shock would cause a heart attack and the man would die.

The minister went to the man's house and said, "Joe, what would you do if you inherited a million dollars?" Joe thought for a moment and said, "Well, Pastor, I think I would give half of it to the church."

The minister fell over dead.

Rahab and Rehob in Rehab

©2001 Jonny Hawkins

🌀 🌀 🌀

A tired minister was at home resting, and through the window he saw a woman approaching his door. She was one of those too-talkative people, and he was not anxious to talk with her. He said to his wife, "I'll just duck upstairs and wait until she goes away."

An hour passed, and then he tiptoed to the stair landing and listened. Not a sound. Starting down the stairs, he called loudly to his wife, "Well, dear, did you get rid of that old bore at last?"

The next moment he heard the voice of the same woman caller, and she couldn't have possibly missed hearing him. Two steps down, he saw them both staring up at him. It seemed truly a crisis moment.

The quick-thinking minister's wife answered. "Yes, dear, she went away over an hour ago. But Mrs. Jones has come to call in the meantime, and I'm sure you'll be glad to greet her."

◎ ◎ ◎

A clergyman had been invited to attend a party of the Sunday school nursery department. He decided to surprise them. Getting on his hands and knees, flipping his coat over his head like wings, he hopped in on all fours, cackling like a bird. Imagine his surprise when he learned that due to a switch in locations he had intruded on the ladies' missionary meeting!

◎ ◎ ◎

Member: How did you like the minister's sermon?

Friend: Frankly, I like our own minister better.

Member: Why is that?

Friend: It's the words they use. Our minister says, "In conclusion," and then he concludes. Your minister says, "Lastly," and he lasts.

"This isn't that kind of boat...there won't be any gambling."

◎　◎　◎

Question: Who can stay single even if he marries many women?

Answer: A minister.

"Mom says never to talk about somebody behind their back...__or__ their front."

©2000 Jonny Hawkins

Miracle

A man asked a priest what a miracle was. A full explanation did not satisfy the man. "Can you give me an example of a miracle?"

"Well," said the priest, "turn around, and I'll see what I can do." As the man did so, he gave him a terrific kick in the seat of his pants.

"Did you feel that?"

"I sure did!"

"Well," said the priest, "it would have been a miracle if you hadn't!"

Model

The young preacher was flattered when someone described him as a "model" preacher.

His pride, however, soon vanished when he turned to his dictionary and found the definition of "model": a small imitation of the real thing.

He was a little more cautious the next time. On being described as a "warm" preacher, he turned to his pocket dictionary, which read, "warm: not so hot."

Monkey

The Bible shows that men made monkeys of themselves, but science claims that monkeys made men of themselves.

Money

A Christian making money fast is just a man in a cloud of dust: it will fill his eyes if he be not careful.

—Charles Spurgeon

Moses

Question: What were Moses' thoughts when he saw the golden calf that Aaron made?

Answer: He had a cow.

ⓢ ⓢ ⓢ

Sunday school teacher: You can be sure that if Moses were alive today, he'd be considered a remarkable man.

Student: He sure ought to be—he'd be more than 2500 years old!

ⓢ ⓢ ⓢ

Question: Why was Moses the most wicked man who ever lived?

Answer: He broke the Ten Commandments all at once.

ⓢ ⓢ ⓢ

Father: What did you learn in Sunday school this morning?

Son: We learned about how Moses went behind enemy lines to rescue the Jews from the Egyptians. Moses ordered the engineers to build a pontoon bridge. After the people crossed, he sent bombers back to blow up the bridge and the Egyptian tanks that were following them. And then . . .

Father: Did your teacher really tell it like that?

Son: No, but if I told you what he said, you would never believe it.

©2000 Jonny Hawkins

"They were all out of sackcloth and ashes."

©2001 Jonny Hawkins

Naomi

Question: What type of personality would Naomi have had if her daughter-in-law had not followed her?

Answer: Ruthless.

Nebuchadnezzar

Question: What did Nebuchadnezzar do when Shadrach, Meshach, and Abednego would not bow down and worship him?

Answer: He had them fired.

⑥ ⑥ ⑥

Question: After his punishment of eating grass for many years, how did King Nebuchadnezzar feel?

Answer: Udderly ridiculous.

Noah

As Noah remarked while the animals were boarding the ark, "Now I herd everything."

⑥ ⑥ ⑥

©2000 Jonny Hawkins

Question: What was Noah's response to everyone that made fun of him building the ark?

Answer: You're all wet.

❀ ❀ ❀

Question: What was Noah's favorite class in school?

Answer: Ark-itecture.

❀ ❀ ❀

A little boy, just back from Sunday school, asked his father if Noah had a wife.

"Of course he did," replied the father. "Her name was Joan of Arc."

ⓖ ⓖ ⓖ

Moses figured they would grow on the world, but at first he was hesitant about allowing Chia Pets aboard.

©2002 Jonny Hawkins

Question: How do we know that Noah had a pig in the ark?

Answer: He had Ham.

⑥ ⑥ ⑥

Question: What special event took place on Mount Ararat?

Answer: Noah parked the ark.

⑥ ⑥ ⑥

Question: What's the difference between Noah's ark and an archbishop?

Answer: One was a high ark, but the other is a hierarch.

⑥ ⑥ ⑥

Question: Where did Noah strike the first nail in the ark?

Answer: On the head.

⑥ ⑥ ⑥

Question: Where did the cock crow when everyone in the world heard him?

Answer: In Noah's ark.

⑥ ⑥ ⑥

Noah tried to teach the donkeys on the ark to steer, but all they did was helm and haw.

Noel

A famous writer once sent Christmas cards containing nothing but 25 letters of the alphabet. When some of his friends admitted that they had failed to understand his message, he pointed to the card and cried, "Look! No 'L'!"

ⓖ ⓖ ⓖ

Notes

A minister preached a very short sermon. He explained, "My dog got into my office and chewed up some of my notes."

At the close of the service a visitor asked, "If your dog ever has pups, may my pastor have one?"

ⓖ ⓖ ⓖ

"You want the Highway to Heaven? Take a right at The Roman's Road to The Narrow Way..."

©2001 Jonny Hawkins

O

Offering

An usher was passing a collection plate at a large church wedding. One of those attending looked up, very puzzled. Without waiting for the question, the usher nodded his head, "I know it's unusual, but the father of the bride requested it."

Oratory

Church member: Pastor, you have a marvelous gift of oratory. How did you develop it?

Pastor: I learned to speak like kids learn to skate or ride a bike—by doggedly making a fool of myself until I got used to it.

"I can't believe there are potholes in the parking lot...I thought they just consecrated it!"

©2002 Jonny Hawkins

P
~~~

Pastor

An elderly woman was weeping as she bade goodbye to the man who had been pastor of her church for several years.

"My dear lady," consoled the departing pastor, "don't get so upset. The bishop surely will send a much better pastor to replace me here."

"That's what they told us the last time," wailed the woman.

The pastor teaches, though he must solicit his own classes. He heals, though without pills or knife. He is sometimes a lawyer, often a social worker, something of an editor, a bit of a philosopher and entertainer, a salesman, a decorative piece for public functions, and he is supposed to be a scholar.

He visits the sick, marries people, buries the dead, labors to console those who sorrow and to admonish those who sin, and he tries to stay sweet when chided for not doing his duty. He plans programs, appoints committees when he can get them, and spends considerable time in keeping people out of each other's hair.

In addition, he prepares a sermon and preaches it on
Sunday to those who don't happen to have any
other engagement. Then on Monday he smiles when
someone roars, "What a job—you only have to
work one day a week!"

Modern-day worship of a golden calf

©2001 Jonny Hawkins

Patience

Patience is the ability to endure something as long as it happens to the other fellow.

Paul

Question: Why did the apostle Paul spend so much time in prison?

Answer: He had an arresting personality.

@ @ @

Question: Why did Paul make so many missionary trips?

Answer: He was born to Rome.

Perfect

Preacher: Does anyone know anyone who is perfect?

Parishioner: My wife's first husband.

Pharaoh

Question: Why didn't Pharaoh let the Israelites go into the wilderness after the first six plagues?

Answer: He was in de Nile.

Phoenicians

Sunday school teacher: What were the Phoenicians famous for?

Sunday school student: Blinds.

Piano Player

A circuit preacher rode into a backwoods town and set up a series of camp meetings. The first evening he asked for a volunteer piano player so the congregation could sing. He promptly got a volunteer and the hymnals were distributed.

"All right," said the preacher. "Let's all sing hymn number 4."

"Sorry, preacher," said the piano player. "I don't know hymn number 4."

"That's OK," said the enthusiastic preacher. "We'll just sing hymn number 27. Everybody knows it."

The piano player squirmed a bit on his bench and said, "Sorry, preacher, I don't know hymn number 27."

The preacher, keeping his good nature, said, "Don't feel badly about it. We'll just sing hymn number 34. Everybody learned that when they were small children."

The piano player was really nervous by now and said, "Sorry, preacher, but I guess I don't know hymn number 34."

Whereupon someone in the back shouted, "That piano player is an idiot!"

"Hold it!" exclaimed the preacher, "I want that man who called the piano player an idiot to stand up."

No one stood.

"If he won't stand up, I want the man sitting beside the man who called the piano player an idiot to stand up."

No one stood.

After a brief period of complete silence, a little fellow in the back stood up and said, "Preacher, I didn't call the piano player an idiot, and I'm not sitting beside the man who called the piano player an idiot. But what I want to know is, who called that idiot a piano player?"

Praise

A notice in the church bulletin read, "The pastor will be gone tonight, and we will be having a service of singing and praise."

Praise the Lord

Did you hear about the country parson who decided to buy a horse? The dealer assured him that the one he selected was a perfect choice.

"This horse," he said, "has lived all his life in a religious atmosphere. So remember that he'll never start to go if you order 'Giddyap.' You've got to say, 'Praise the Lord.' Likewise, a 'Whoa' will never make him stop. You've got to say, 'Amen.'"

Thus forewarned, the parson paid for the horse, mounted him, and, with a cheery "Praise the Lord," sent him wandering off in the direction of the parson's parish.

Suddenly, however, he noticed that the road ahead had been washed out, leaving a chasm two hundred feet deep. In a panic, he forgot his instructions and cried, "Whoa!" in vain several times. The horse continued to run forward. At the very last moment he remembered to cry, "Amen." The horse stopped short at the very brink of the chasm. But alas! That's when the parson, out of force of habit, murmured fervently, "Praise the Lord!"

Growing up Samson

©2001 Jonny Hawkins

Prayer

I don't believe in all this contemporary language in church. Somehow I can't ever see myself saying, "Our Dad, who art in heaven."

ⓖ ⓖ ⓖ

A youngster was overheard praying, "Dear God, we had a good time at church today. I wish you could have been there."

ⓖ ⓖ ⓖ

If prayers were puddings, many men would starve.

ⓖ ⓖ ⓖ

Sunday school teacher: What is prayer?

Sunday school student: That's a message sent to God at night and on Sundays, when the rates are lower.

ⓖ ⓖ ⓖ

A bedtime prayer: "I'm not praying for anything for myself . . . just a new bike for my brother that we both can ride."

ⓖ ⓖ ⓖ

"You can set my tail on fire, Samson, but please include my name in Foxe's Book of Martyrs."

Many who pray on their knees on Sunday prey on their friends the rest of the week.

⚙ ⚙ ⚙

Little Billy knelt beside his bed and prayed, "Dear God, if You can find some way to put the vitamins in candy and ice cream instead of in spinach and cod liver oil, I would sure appreciate it. Amen."

⚙ ⚙ ⚙

A hungry little boy was beginning to eat his dinner when his father reminded him that they hadn't prayed.

"We don't have to," said the little boy. "Mommy is a good cook!"

⚙ ⚙ ⚙

Little Susie concluded her prayer by saying, "Dear God, before I finish, please take care of Daddy, Mommy, my baby brother, Grandma, and Grandpa ...and please, God, take care of Yourself or else we're all sunk!"

⚙ ⚙ ⚙

"Something's fishy. Judas is wanting to start a Disciples' Union...and he wants to be treasurer."

©2001 Jonny Hawkins

❡ ❡ ❡

The pastor visited the Sunday evening youth group, and he asked for volunteers to pray. A little girl volunteered to pray for the pastor. Her prayer: "Be with our pastor, and help him to preach a better sermon next Sunday."

Sarah has a mid-laugh crisis.

©2000 Jonny Hawkins

Nowadays the only time people seem to get on their knees is when they're looking for a contact lens.

A teacher handed out a test and told the children they could start answering the questions.

She noticed little Billy sitting with his head bowed, his hands over his face. She approached him.

"Don't you feel well?" she inquired.

"Oh, I'm fine, teacher. Maybe it's unconstitutional, but I always pray before a test!"

@ @ @

Little Timmy was saying his prayers one night. His mother overheard this entreaty: "And please make Tommy stop throwing things at me. By the way, I've mentioned this before."

@ @ @

After a family disturbance, one of the little boys closed his bedtime prayer by saying, "And please don't give my dad any more children . . . He doesn't know how to treat the ones he already has."

@ @ @

An ocean liner was sinking, and the captain yelled, "Does anybody know how to pray?"

A minister on board said, "I do."

"Good," said the captain. "You start praying. The rest of us will put on the life jackets. We're one belt short."

"I can tell by your wood, hay, and stubble that you
haven't shaved and showered in days."

©2002 Jonny Hawkins

Preacher

One overly enthusiastic young preacher encouraged his listeners to be filled with fresh veal and new zigor.

🌀 🌀 🌀

The test of a preacher is that his congregation goes away saying not "What a lovely sermon" but "I will do something!"

—St. Francis de Sales

🌀 🌀 🌀

A little boy in church, awaking after a nap, asked his father, "Has the preacher finished?"

"Yes, son, he has finished, but he hasn't stopped talking."

🌀 🌀 🌀

Dwight L. Moody stopped to visit with a fellow clergyman. The friend told Moody he would love to have him address his congregation, but that it would probably be embarrassing. The congregation was in the habit of walking out before a sermon was finished—no matter who the preacher was.

Moody said he would be delighted to take his chances and thought he would be able to hold them there until the end.

On Sunday morning, Moody mounted the pulpit and began by pointing out that the first half of his sermon would be addressed to the sinners and the last half to the saints in the congregation. All stayed to the end.

ⓖ ⓖ ⓖ

A preacher was called upon to substitute for the regular minister, who was stranded in a snowstorm. The speaker began by explaining the meaning of a substitute. "If you break a window," he said, "and then place a cardboard there instead, that is a substitute."

After the sermon, a woman who had listened intently shook hands with him, and wishing to compliment him, said, "You were no substitute . . . you were a real pane!"

Preaching

One Sunday a farmer went to church. When he entered, he saw that he and the preacher were the only ones present. The preacher asked the farmer if he wanted him to go ahead and preach. The farmer said, "I'm not too smart, but if I went to feed my cattle and only one showed up, I'd feed him." So the minister began his sermon.

One hour passed, then two hours, then two and a half hours. The preacher finally finished and came down to ask the farmer how he had liked the sermon.

The farmer answered slowly, "I'm not too smart, but if I went to feed my cattle and only one showed up, I sure wouldn't feed him all the hay."

Priests

Question: What was the favorite clothing worn by the priests?

Answer: Levis.

Procrastination

After hearing his dad preach on justification, sanctification, and all the other -ations, a minister's son was ready when his Sunday school teacher asked if anybody knew what "procrastination" meant. "I'm not sure what it means," he said, "but I know our church believes in it."

Prodigal Son

A little boy told the story of the Prodigal Son for his Sunday school class:

"He sold his coat to buy food, he sold his shirt to buy food, he sold his undershirt to buy food, and then he came to himself."

Proverb

Proverbs: The wisdom of many and the wit of one.

Psychiatric Hotline

Welcome to the Psychiatric Hotline for Ministerial Referral.

If you are obsessive-compulsive, please press 1 repeatedly.

If you are co-dependent, please ask someone to press 2 for you.

If you have multiple personalities, please press 3, 4, 5, 6, and 7.

If you are a schizophrenic, listen carefully, and a small, quiet voice will tell you which number to press.

If you are manic-depressive, it doesn't matter which number you press. No one will answer.

If you have paranoid delusions, we know who you are and what you want. Just stay on the line so we can trace the call.

Thank you for calling the Psychiatric Hotline.

Polygamy

A Mormon acquaintance once pushed Mark Twain into an argument on the issue of polygamy. After long and tedious expositions justifying the practice, the Mormon demanded that Twain cite any passage of Scripture expressly forbidding polygamy.

"Nothing easier," Twain replied. "'No man can serve two masters.'"

"I got it back during the hula hoop craze."

Publican

The seventh grade lesson dealt with the publican and the sinner. The teacher asked the class, "What is a publican?"

One of the students responded, "A publican is opposite of a democrat."

Push

A minister rushed down to the train station every single day to watch the Sunset Limited go by. There was no chore he wouldn't interrupt to carry out his ritual. Members of his congregation deemed his eccentricity juvenile and frivolous and asked him to give it up.

"No, gentlemen," he said firmly. "I preach your sermons, teach your Sunday school, bury your dead, marry you, run your charities, and chairman every drive you conduct. I won't give up seeing that Southern Pacific train every day. I love it! It's the only thing in this town I don't have to push!"

R

Reaping

The chaplain was passing through the prison garment factory.

"Sewing?" he said to a prisoner who was at work.

"No, chaplain," replied the prisoner gloomily, "reaping!"

Religion

Still religion, like water, is the first to freeze.

ⓢ ⓢ ⓢ

Many people treat their religion as a spare tire—they never use it except in an emergency.

Repeating

The new minister stood at the church door greeting parishioners as they departed after the services. The people were generous in complimenting the clergyman for his sermon, except one fellow who said to him, "Pretty dull sermon, Reverend." And in a minute or two the same man appeared again in line and said, "Pretty dull sermon, Reverend." Once again the man appeared, this time muttering, "You really didn't say anything at all, Reverend."

When he got the opportunity, the minister pointed out the triple-threat pest to one of the deacons and inquired about him. "Oh, don't let that guy bother you," said the deacon. "He's a poor soul who goes around repeating whatever he hears other people saying."

❂ ❂ ❂

If Jacob had dreamed of the corporate ladder

©2001 Jonny Hawkins

Reputation

A reputation once broken may possibly be repaired,
but the world will always keep their eyes on the
spot where the crack was.

—Joseph Hall

Riddle

Question: Who is the smallest man in the Bible?

Answer: Some people believe that it was Zaccheaus.
Others believe it was Knee-high-amiah, or Bildad,
the Shoe-hite. But in reality it was Peter—he slept
on his watch!

Question: Where was deviled ham mentioned in the
Bible?

Answer: When the evil spirits entered the swine.

Question: When is high finance first mentioned in the
Bible?

Answer: When Pharaoh's daughter took a little
prophet from the bulrushes.

ɕ ɕ ɕ

Question: Who was the most popular actor in the Bible?

Answer: Samson. He brought the house down.

ⓢ ⓢ ⓢ

Question: Who was Round John Virgin?

Answer: One of the twelve opossums.

ⓢ ⓢ ⓢ

Question: When did Moses sleep with five people in one bed?

Answer: When he slept with his forefathers.

Ruth

Question: When did Ruth treat Boaz badly?

Answer: When she pulled his ears and stepped on his corn.

Sacred

The minister's new secretary, a former worker in the Pentagon, was busily reorganizing her boss's filing system. She labeled one drawer "Sacred" and the other "Top Sacred."

Salary

Three boys were talking about how much money their fathers made.

The lawyer's son said, "My father goes into court on a case and often comes home with as much as $1500 a day."

The doctor's son said, "My father performs an operation and sometimes earns as much as $2000 for it."

The minister's son, determined not to be outdone, said, "That's nothing. My father preaches for 20 minutes on Sunday morning, and it takes six men to carry the money."

Samaritan

Question: What was the giveaway to the Samaritan woman that Jesus was not an ordinary man?

Answer: He knew her too "well."

Samson

Question: What simple affliction brought about the
  death of Samson?

Answer: Fallen arches.

ⓖ ⓖ ⓖ

Question: What happened to Samson's strength?

Answer: It vanished into thin hair.

Sarcasm

Sarcasm is the language of the devil.

—Thomas Carlyle

ⓖ ⓖ ⓖ

Sarcasm comes from the Greek word that means to "rip
  flesh like dogs," or "to gnash the teeth in rage."

Satan

Beware of Satan or evil have his way.

Saul

Question: What caused King Saul to offer sacrifices
  when Samuel was late?

Answer: His alter ego.

Pastor Ferdinand misinterprets II Corinthians 13:12 and greets the brethren with a *Hershey* Kiss.

©2002 Jonny Hawkins

Sermon

The sermon you enjoy most is not likely to be the one that will do you the most good.

🌀   🌀   🌀

Willie got very tired of the long sermon at church. He whispered loudly to his mother, "If we give him the money now, will he let us go out?"

Sermons are like babies: easy to conceive but hard to deliver.

Bible times yo-yo

©2002 Jonny Hawkins

A pastor returned from vacation and asked a
     parishioner, "How did the assistant pastor do
     Sunday morning?"

"It was a poor sermon. Nothing in it at all."

The pastor decided to ask the assistant about it: "How
     did it go Sunday morning?"

"I didn't have time to prepare anything myself, so I
     preached one of your sermons."

◎ ◎ ◎

An old farmer went to church alone. When he
     returned, his wife asked,

"Was the sermon good?"

"Yes."

"What was it about?" persisted his wife.

"Sin."

"Well, what did he say?"

"He was against it."

◎ ◎ ◎

A sermon should have a good beginning and a good
     ending, and they should be as close together as
     possible.

—George Burns

◎ ◎ ◎

First member: I thought the sermon was divine. It reminded me of the peace of God: It passed all understanding.

Second member: It reminded me of the mercies of God: I thought it would endure forever.

☙ ☙ ☙

A new preacher had just begun his sermon. He was a little nervous, and about ten minutes into the talk his mind went blank. He remembered what they had taught him in seminary when a situation like this would arise—repeat your last point. Often this would help you remember what is coming next. So he thought he would give it a try.

"Behold, I come quickly," he said. Still his mind was blank. He tried again. "Behold, I come quickly." Still nothing.

He tried one more time with such force that he fell forward, knocking the pulpit to one side, tripping over the flower pot, and falling into the lap of a little old lady in the front row.

The young preacher apologized and tried to explain what happened. "That's all right, young man," said the little old lady. "It was my fault. I should have gotten out of the way. You told me three times you were coming!"

Shadow

Sin and her shadow, death.

—Milton

Paul bound his letters in genuine Corinthian leather.

©2001 Jonny Hawkins

Shepherds

Question: Which Old Testament book was written by shepherds?

Answer: Lamb-entations.

Sick Woman

The minister's little daughter was sent to bed with a stomachache and missed her usual romp with her daddy. A few minutes later she appeared at the top of the stairs and called to her mother, "Mama, let me talk with Daddy."

"No, my dear, not tonight. Get back in bed."

"Please, Mama."

"I said, 'no.' That's enough now."

"Mother, I'm a very sick woman, and I must see my pastor."

@ @ @

Sin

The wages of sin have no deductions.

ⓖ ⓖ ⓖ

How candid we are in confessing other people's sins.

ⓖ ⓖ ⓖ

A Sunday school teacher asked a little girl, "What are the sins of omission?"

After some thought, she answered: "They're the sins we ought to have committed but haven't."

Skates

Question: Why is a pair of skates like the forbidden fruit in the Garden of Eden?

Answer: Both come before the fall.

Sleep

"How late do you usually sleep on Sunday morning?"

"It all depends."

"Depends on what?"

"The length of the sermon."

ⓖ ⓖ ⓖ

Jack: Do you know Pete Wilson?

Mack: I sure do. We slept in the same church for over 15 years.

Smaller

The smaller we are, the more room we have for God.

Sodom and Gomorrah

Sunday school teacher: What were Dan and Beersheba?

Sunday school student: I think they were husband and wife, almost like Sodom and Gomorrah.

◎ ◎ ◎

God's destruction of the wicked cities of Sodom and Gomorrah is a story that makes a vivid impression. A teacher relating the story to her class was saying, "Lot was warned to take his wife and flee out of the city, which was about to be destroyed. Lot got away safely, but his wife looked back and was turned to a pillar of salt. Now, children, do you have any questions to ask about this story?"

A boy raised his hand. "What happened to the flea?"

Solomon

"King Solomon," declared a little girl in Sunday school, "is my favorite character in the Bible. He was kind to ladies and animals."

The startled teacher asked, "Who told you that?"

"Nobody told me. I read it myself in the Bible," asserted the little girl. "It says Solomon kept seven hundred wives and three hundred porcupines."

☺ ☺ ☺

©2001 Jonny Hawkins

Question: Why was Solomon the wisest man in the world?

Answer: Because he had so many wives to advise him.

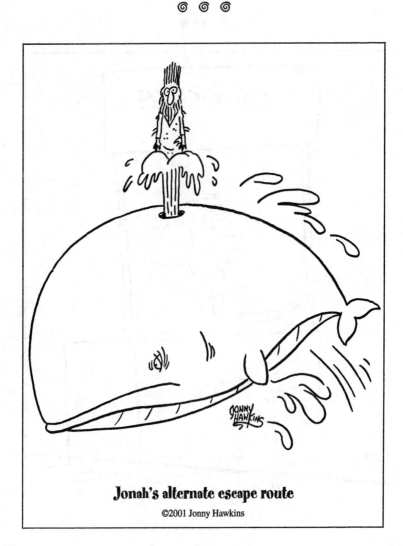

Jonah's alternate escape route

©2001 Jonny Hawkins

Sound

A husband, unable to attend church on a Sunday
    morning when a preacher was candidating for the
    pulpit, asked his wife, "Was he sound?"

She replied, "He was all sound!"

Stained Glass

A three-year-old boy gazed in delight at the handsome
    stained glass windows in a church and told his
    mother, "Look—cartoons!"

Straight and Narrow

The problem with following the straight and narrow
    path is that you so seldom meet anybody you know.

Stumbling Block

You can't build a church with stumbling blocks.

St. Peter

St. Peter looked at the new arrival skeptically; he had
    no advance knowledge of his coming.

"How did you get here?" asked Peter.

"Flu."

Sunday

An elderly lady, when asked to give her opinion of her
    pastor, said that on six days a week he was invisible,
    and on the seventh he was incomprehensible.

☺ ☺ ☺

Little Raymond came home from church beaming. He
rushed up the stairs and yelled, "Mommy, Mommy!
Father Alonzo said something nice about me in his
prayers this morning! He said, 'O Lord, we thank
Thee for our food and Raymond.'"

Sunday School

The Sunday school teacher had just concluded a talk
on the creation account in Genesis when one of the
children said, "My father says we are descended
from monkeys."

"After class," replied the teacher, "we will discuss
your private family problems."

☺ ☺ ☺

"Mommy," said little Judy, "did you ever see a cross-
eyed bear?"

"Why, no, Judy" chuckled her mother, "but why do you
ask?"

"Well, in church we sang, 'Gladly, the cross-eyed bear.'"

☺ ☺ ☺

A Sunday school teacher asked a little girl if she said
her prayers every night.

"No, not every night," declared the child, "because
some nights I don't want anything!"

©2002 Jonny Hawkins

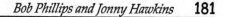

A little boy forgot his lines in a Sunday school presentation. His mother was in the front row to prompt him. She gestured and formed the words silently with her lips, but it did not help. Her son's memory was blank.

Finally, she leaned forward and whispered the cue, "I am the light of the world."

The child beamed and with great feeling and a loud clear voice said, "My mother is the light of the world."

"Where's the concordance?"

©2001 Jonny Hawkins

☉ ☉ ☉

Sunday school teacher: Why did Jesus know the
   Scriptures so well?

Student: That's easy. His Daddy wrote them.

☉ ☉ ☉

Sunday school teacher: Who were the twin boys in the
   Bible?

Student: That's easy. First and Second Samuel!

⑥ ⑥ ⑥

Sunday school teacher: Which parable in the Bible do you like best?

Student: The one about the guy that loafs and fishes.

⑥ ⑥ ⑥

"Daddy, I want to ask you a question," said little Bobby after his first day in Sunday school.

"Yes, Bobby, what is it?"

"The teacher was reading the Bible to us—all about the children of Israel building the temple, the children of Israel crossing the Red Sea, the children of Israel making sacrifices. Didn't the grown-ups do anything?"

⑥ ⑥ ⑥

A little boy asked his Sunday school teacher, "Is it true shepherds have dirty socks?"

"What do you mean?" the teacher asked.

"I heard that the shepherds washed their socks by night."

⑥ ⑥ ⑥

A little boy was writing the memory verse for the day on the blackboard: Do one to others as others do one to you.

          ⓢ ⓢ ⓢ

A little boy came home from Sunday school and told his mother that they had just learned a new song about a boy named Andy. His mother couldn't understand what he meant until he sang the song.

"Andy walks with me, Andy talks with me.

Andy tells me I am his own . . . "

T

Temper

Church member: That's what I like about playing golf with you, Pastor—when your golf ball goes into the rough, you don't swear.

Pastor: That may be true, but where I spit, the grass dies!

Temptation

"Opportunity knocks only once," one preacher warned his flock, "but temptation bangs on your door for years."

Tennis

Question: Where is tennis mentioned in the Bible?

Answer: When Joseph served in Pharaoh's court.

Ten Commandments

If God believed in permissiveness, He would have given us the Ten Suggestions.

If tennis shoes existed in Bible times

©2002 Jonny Hawkins

Toastmaster

Member: Pastor, a friend of mine died, and I would like you to speak at his burial service.

Pastor: Where is he going to be buried?

Member: Oh, he is going to be cremated.

Pastor: You don't want a speaker—what you need is a toastmaster!

©2001 Jonny Hawkins

Tongue

Once when Charles Spurgeon, then a young man, was passing by the house of a woman with a poison tongue, she let him have a volley of impolite words.

"Yes, thank you; I am quite well," Spurgeon said.

Then she let out another volley.

"Yes, it does look as if it's going to rain," he replied.

Surprised, the woman exclaimed, "Bless the man, he's deaf as a post! What's the use of talking to him?"

Tower of Babel

Question: What was the Tower of Babel?

Answer: That was where Solomon kept his wives.

Tract

Jehovah's Witnesses have tract me down!

Troubles

A kindly country parson who had just married a young couple had a parting word for the groom: "Son, God bless you. You're at the end of all your troubles."

A year later, the groom returned to the scene and moaned. "What a year I've gone through! And you're the man who told me I was at the end of my troubles."

"So I did, son," smiled the parson. "I just didn't tell you which end."

"As a former royal steed from Rome, I much prefer a Caesar salad."

©2002 Jonny Hawkins

**One of the apostle Paul's ironic
untold stories**

©2002 Jonny Hawkins

Truth

Truth may be stretched, but cannot be broken, and
  always gets above falsehood as oil does above
  water.

—Miguel Cervantes

Tweedle

A minister named Tweedle reluctantly refused a
  Doctor of Divinity degree. He said that he'd
  rather be Tweedle dum than Tweedle, D.D.

Twenty-Third Psalm

A lot of church members know the Twenty-Third
  Psalm much better than they know the Shepherd.

ⓖ ⓖ ⓖ

A three-year-old's version of the Twenty-Third Psalm:
  "He leadeth me beside distilled water."

Typewriter

"I operate a typewriter by the biblical system."
"What is that?"
"Seek-and-ye-shall-find."

"The same as I think of your personalized chariot plates—vanity, vanity, all is vanity."

©2002 Jonny Hawkins

U
~~~

Umpires

The devil challenged St. Peter to a baseball game.

"How can you win, Satan?" asked St. Peter. "All the famous ballplayers are up here."

"How can I lose?" answered Satan. "All the umpires are down here."

Unbeliever

An unbeliever sneered, "So many things in the world are made wrong. Look at that little acorn on that big tree and that big pumpkin on that little vine! People talk about an all-wise God at the head of this universe. Now if I had been doing it, I would have put that acorn on the vine, and the pumpkin on the oak."

Just then an acorn fell and hit him on the head.

Usher

The retiring usher was instructing his youthful successor in the details of his office. "And remember, we have nothing but good, kind Christians in this church—until you try to put someone else in their pew."

"For the last time...we're not building it for the purpose of bungee jumping!"

©2001 Jonny Hawkins

Vanity

A young girl went to her pastor and confessed that she feared she had incurred the sin of vanity.

"What makes you think that?" asked the minister.

"Because every morning when I look in the mirror, I think how beautiful I am."

"That isn't a sin," was the reassuring reply. "It's only a mistake."

Veil

A minister married a couple. The woman had on a veil, and he could not see her face. After the ceremony, the man asked the minister, "How much do I owe you?"

"No charge," replied the minister.

"But I want to show my appreciation." So the man gave him 50 cents.

About that time the bride pulled off her veil, and the minister, looking at the bride, gave the man 25 cents change.

Voice

The choir had come out of rehearsal.

"Do you do a lot of singing at home?" Bill asked Roy, a fellow choir member.

"Yes, I sing a lot. I use my voice just to kill time," said Roy.

Bill nodded. "You certainly have a fine weapon."

ⓖ ⓖ ⓖ

"We love because He first loved us."

©2000 Jonny Hawkins

Wicked

Deacon: It says here, "The wicked flee when no man pursueth."

Pastor: Yes, that's true, but they make much better time when somebody is after them.

Wickedness

The way to wickedness is always through wickedness.

—Seneca

Worse

A pastor always used the phrase, "It might be worse," when some calamity would come his way.

One day a friend said to him, "I've something to tell you, and you won't be able to use your favorite phrase. I dreamed last night that I died and went to hell."

"It might be worse," said the preacher.

"How could it be worse?"

"It might be true."

Nature bears testimony of God.

©2001 Jonny Hawkins

Zacchaeus

Question: What kind of person cooked the meal for Jesus when he had dinner with Zacchaeus?

Answer: A short-order cook.

Other Books by Bob Phillips

For more information, send a self-addressed stamped envelope to:

Family Services
P.O. Box 9363
Fresno, California 93702